WHY WE CAN'T FIX UNEMPLOYMENT: An Anthology

By

Jim Green

DEDICATED TO:

Our creating a more civilized world, and Our Youth, who will have to live in the world we have left them with….

ISBN-13: 978-1496032935

ISBN-10: 1496032934

PROLOGUE

This is my 14th book, and my last….published my first on my 78th birthday [from materials gathering dust over the past 30 years]…but before I get too deep into the purpose of this book…I want to say a few word about people who "write".

First, it is an addiction….probably akin to drug addiction, or alcoholism…of course, persons who write hope others will read what they have written, and find of interest, better yet—but whether anyone reads what they have to say is irrelevant to the compulsion to write….

My suspicion is that every person who writes books, or newspaper editors, etc., are afflicted with the writing bug—and like the Columnist—daily or weekly—when we wake up, or at random times, we are formulating in the background, thoughts for the words we want to commit from pen to paper. And this book is no exception.

Also, almost every person I have met who is afflicted with this malady are never quite satisfied with what they have written, and find themselves tinkering around the edges—almost up to the minute of publication. A good example is the early release of President Obama's 2014 State of the Union address—with hardly a paragraph escaping some penciled in revision.

Someone said [wish I could recall who, to give credit] that we move from being a "writer", to being an "author" --when people start reading what we have written. And in spite of the unrelenting compulsion to write—we are always hoping we are writing the next "Gone With The Wind".

For instance, with just the title, alone, on my first book—and in spite of the difficulty in writing about a sad and deeply personal matter—a true story-- in which I was stripped of my rights as a U.S. citizen—by a Hitler Youth— and involved criminal negligence on the part of the government defendants, in a civil rights action, in the death of our son, and which current sitting justice on the U.S. Supreme Court, Anthony Kennedy, covered up---but with just the title I thought it would create a particular interest—THE

HARVARD BOYS CLUB. It was never about the money, for any of my books—but it is a rude awakening for new authors—people don't buy books they are unaware exist....

And with the market now flooded with eBooks—it is only a tiny fraction that get exposure, and the secret—the experts tell me—is to find a niche for your book. That is, wide exposure is exceedingly rare—but this is not a "poor me" session—just the reality— and the self-pleasure in writing, may be its only reward—and for most with this addiction, I suspect, pleasure enough....

The thorn in my side—and the motivation for most of my books—is the "Big Lie" in America. The lie that we are looking for an answer to pervasive unemployment....it is BS!

And the truth is: Every politician espouses their motivation to create jobs, but the truth is, we do not have a *single* program *specific* to address unemployment as a "stand alone social problem"!

Indeed, Republican job creation is willing to sacrifice millions of Americans so we can hold in place myths that no longer work in a 21st Century economy—and the purpose of this book is to take the reader on a journey…an odyssey to explore the reason for this…Like Christy's bridge scandal, most of what Republicans are doing, today, defies all rational human thought, but then…

A puzzlement for me—with the economy in meltdown in 2009—and losing 500,000 plus jobs a month at the beginning of the Obama administration—why on earth did anyone in their right mind think HR 2847, the HIRE Act—would work?

The HIRE Act is based on the premise: Fix the market, and this will in turn fix unemployment—when the mind-set should have been the exact opposite—Fix unemployment, and this will fix the market [more on this shortly].

The Democrats had a very narrow window in 2009, to end unemployment in America—permanently—they had on the books the "legal authority" to limit our unemployment to "3%"— i.e., at no time, and to this day, should our unemployment in America exceed 3%!

The primary reason we are unable to fix unemployment, however, is because we are not honest about what we are doing now, specifically:

Unemployment is a "social" problem—a serious "social" problem—sometimes with dire consequences—when I got out of the Navy, I moved to Washington D.C.—from Kansas—I took an apartment along with many other young singles—pretty much to party, party, party....

But it was not all party for one fellow who had recently been fired [Dwayne Dyer observed that even the word "fired" sounds like some kind of medieval ritual], and his wife and children left him. He came to D.C. to drink himself to death.

He moved in with a case of Vodka, and three weeks later, apparently when the Vodka ran out, they found him dead—he broke the last bottle and stabbed himself in the stomach.

We are reported to have 12 million unemployed Americans, as I write—and while it seems improbable few result in this kind of dire ending—divorce is not infrequent in long-term unemployment—and when the Department of Labor reports that the unemployment rate has gone down—it is not, solely, because employment has gone up, but rather because tens of thousands have stopped looking for work…or are…..

The larger point being raised, here, is that we have an extremely serious "social" problem in unemployment—but, as noted, we do not have a _single_ program _specific_ to address the social consequences of this problem—_and we need to start asking why_?

For instance, and to clarify—when the CDC became aware of the AIDS virus, they immediately set out to end this dread disease, and "social" problem—but when it comes to unemployment we cling to the _myth_ that the market can provide anybody wanting a job, with a job—it is BS— and it is a "social" problem that will get even worse as we advance into the 21st Century....

As a result of automation, alone "public-sector" employees are an _indispensable_ component to the _effective_ functioning of a modern market economy—both now, and growing exponentially as we advance into the 21st Century.

And we have the "legal authority" in America to put this paradigm into effect, tomorrow....

But, it is also a fact that Washington is petrified, on the basis of flat-world thinking, and McCarthyism—to enforce this "legal authority"—and they are willing to undermine—what they claim to seek—a robust and viable market economy—rather than change!

Manufacturing is disappearing in America, to whatever degree, because people do not buy the products manufactured for the market—when they are unemployed....

86% of Americans believe that "anybody willing to work should be able to find a job"—so there is no lack of political will on the part of the American people to end our unemployment crisis—so we must look elsewhere….and the purpose of this book is to sort that out.

Again, we sacrifice millions of Americans so the "market" can maintain, as defined in the metaphor-- A POOL OF SLAVES: To Be Used And Discarded "at will" [on Amazon/Kindle]—And this is premised on a *fraud*: The market can provide anybody wanting a job, with a job. It is BS!

To understand the distinction— Humphrey-Hawkins said "unemployment" is a serious "social" problem—and here is the "legal authority" to end it—but the truth is, we have no such "stand-alone" solution to end unemployment, at present—ALL of our current solutions are based on the _fraud,_ above! And, of course, if the market fails, the unemployed are out of luck!

The truth is, save for only one year in the middle of WW II, we have not had anything even approaching full employment over the past century— and, since the advent of corporations....

What constitutes "Full Employment" is all over the map among economists, and ranges from 0 to 9%--and while almost every politician advocates for "Full Employment" –the truth is, and to reiterate, we do not have a _single_ program _specific_ to end our unemployment crisis, in America!

Ending unemployment is _not_ on the table!

And the really sad part of this truism is the _myth_ that we need a pool of slaves—a mind-set which, in fact, _undermines_ the market! It doesn't work in a 21st Century economy!

The market thrives when we have a robust, employed, consuming workforce—and
I tried to sum up the duality of this dilemma in the title: FULL EMPLOYMENT IS A PRO-MARKET CONCEPT

In case it is not absolutely clear up to now--I love capitalism. I am an unabashed supporter of: build a better widget, sell it for a million bucks, and retire in South Florida. But when every waking moment in capitalism is spent pondering how to eliminate as many of us humans, as possible, from the workplace—to increase profits—

WHY on earth would anyone in their right mind look to capitalism to solve a "social" problem that is antithetical to its objective?

Employment/Unemployment relate to social issues—The market/capitalism is not in the social work business, and would soon be out of business if they were—

Even disregarding the highly erratic nature of the market--It is not a stable place to look to solve unemployment, particularly given a 50% failure rate in start-ups.

So why do we cling to the model: fix the market, and this will in turn fix unemployment, rather than fix unemployment, and this will fix the market?

What we are doing now is a lose-lose proposition—the unemployed lose, and the market loses....

The balance of this book is based on the above, and hopefully to clarify—refine. The reader may not agree—but my objective is not "political" in the ideologue since—but rather my objective is to "problem-solve"--to lay out the facts regarding the most pernicious social problem facing America, today: Pervasive Unemployment—as Oscar Wilde averred "The only truly worthless opinion, is an unbiased one"—but it is key, here, that "opinion" is backed up with "facts".

The following are letters to President Obama, letters to the editor, papers written on the subject at hand, FACEFOOK postings, etc., again to refine the above. Also, apologize for some duplication [look for the nuggets in the redundancy…lol]…also, if you are a typo freak you will probably not like my writing….just look for content…THX

Bio Info:
http://www.amazon.com/James-L.-Jim-Green/e/B001KHZIMM/ref=ntt_dp_e pwbk_0

CHAPTER ONE

President Obama/Council of Economic Advisers:

I am writing to urge you to re-classify Pot via Executive Order—and place in same category as alcohol. When we now spend more locking people up, than we spend on educating our youth—[even disregarding the cost of interdiction]---and 50% of those we have locked up in for drug related offenses—i.e., we need "medical" rather than "criminal" solutions.

The primary reason I am writing, however, regards the most pernicious social problem facing America, today [inter-related with the above]: Pervasive Unemployment.

And quite by accident I came across an explanation for our inability to solve this problem—the "belief" that the market can provide anybody wanting a job, with a job.

The data doesn't support this—it hasn't been true since the mid-1970's, and on the basis of automation, alone, it becomes exponentially less true as we advance into the 21st Century.

Further, according to the CBO, on our current path it will be 2017 before we return to even an anemic 5.5%, with unemployment benefits long since expired [and in jeopardy, now]—and if the market fails, the unemployed are out of luck.

The puzzlement for me—when we have the "legal authorization" [15

USC § 3101] to limit our unemployment to 3%--[a Pro-Market solution]--Why on earth would Larry Summers [the consensus in 2009] be to apply anachronistic economic theory: Fix the market, and this will in turn fix unemployment—rather than—fix unemployment, and this will fix the market?

High unemployment/sluggish recovery is not a non sequitur, and a retaliatory electorate in 2010 [we didn't fix unemployment], ushered in a House full of lunatics!

Representative Conyers is the lone Congressman who advocates for implementation of Humphrey-Hawkins [HR 870], and I am writing to urge you to explore this, or a like methodology, for solving our unemployment crisis.

For instance, The Neighbor-To-Neighbor Job Creation Act [hereafter NTN]: A federally mandated, Social Insurance, owned by our employed, to provide a fund to hire/train our unemployed. For a modest 4% of salary policy cost we can create more "private-sector" jobs in 6 months, than our current path [HR 2847], in 6 years. Further, this has strong political support—86% of Americans believe "anybody willing to work, should be able to find a job".

With highest regards,

Jim Green, Democrat opponent to Lamar Smith, Congress, 2000

CHAPTER TWO

To the Editor: The NEW YORKER

ECONOMIC INCLUSIVISM: A Pro-Market Solution For Our Unemployment Crisis [what we are doing now is Anti-Employment, and Anti-Market]

Pope Francis has presented us with a challenge for social and economic justice—but until we get honest about the "Belief" that is preventing us from moving into our 21st Century economy…here and throughout the OECD [the market-driven economies, including the U.S.]--both the jobless and the market will suffer.

During the 2008 election the electorate spoke loud and clear—*Fix*

Unemployment. With majorities in both the Senate and House, I thought the Democrats would employ Public Law 15 USC § 3101, which provided them with the "Legal Authorization" to limit our unemployment to "3%". In short, at no time should our unemployment in America exceed "3%".

To my dismay—the Democrats opted for 1950's economic theory, with employment now being restored at a snail's pace, and the result has been a disaster [I believe the 2010 election was retaliation for not fixing unemployment, and also ushered in a House full of lunatics]!

The Democrats would have had broad public support in 2010 with 3% unemployment, and now that is in jeopardy for 10 years, and it left us with a Washington in paralysis.

Also, according to the CBO, on our current path, it will be 2017 for us to get back to even an anemic 5.5%, with unemployment benefits long since expired—[the House Republicans are threatening not to renew the current rollover, as I write]--and if the market fails, the jobless are out of luck....

The puzzlement for me is why would our brightest and best make such a critical error? The solution to a problem is measured by results—and the data, alone, shows this result to be miserable.

Further, this is not limited to our leaders in America—and is also true throughout the OECD, with Eurozone 12.1%, as I write, and 25% in Greece and Spain, common. I would add that I believe all of these leaders are genuinely concerned with fixing joblessness.

So, I ask, why do our leaders keep applying 1950's economic theory, in a 21st Century economy—particularly, given the most serious social problem facing us today, widespread unemployment?

And my take is because it is based on a pervasive, but false, "Belief":

THE "BELIEF" THAT THE MARKET CAN PROVIDE ANYBODY WANTING A JOB, WITH A JOB —[and our market economies stand on one foot and then the other waiting on the market to solve a problem it is INCAPABLE of solving--more on this shortly—this

"Belief" is bedrock for Republicans(1), and let's not forget that pervasive belief once had it that the world was flat]....

And thus the policies and laws to solve unemployment, in our market-driven economies, have been framed around, and based on this "Belief"....and it cannot be disregarded, what psychologists call "groupness"—a circle the wagons mind-set by vested interests to preserve the status quo—for instance by President Obama's Council of Economic Advisers, and their counterparts in the OECD.

Also, many in the "rank and file" have so bought into the myth that ONLY the market can create jobs—they have joined with the 1% who deny climate change to justify drilling the Rockies down to an anthill---to assure their having a job—the planet be dam--ed!]….

But, this hasn't been true since the mid-1970's, and "High and persistent unemployment has pervaded almost every OECD country since the mid-1970's", according to Dr. William F. Mitchell, and every credible economist [and pervasive unemployment dominates our news programs daily].

What happened in the mid-1970's, as the result of a Grotian Moment-like paradigm shift in the world economy, is open to debate—I believe it was the result of the converging forces of automation, globalization, technology, etc., reaching a critical mass in the mid-1970's—i.e., we became victims of our success, and since, we have celebrated automation in the workplace, and then got a "deer in the headlights" regarding the displaced employee [a problem which left uncorrected, will grow exponentially as we advance into the 21st Century]. In the U.S. we defined the impact of this economic shift as "malaise".

A factor apparently not considered throughout the OECD is that unemployment is a "social" problem, with serious social consequences—We, as societies, have the responsibility to solve….and when every waking moment in capitalism is spent pondering how to eliminate as many of us humans, as possible, from the workplace—to increase profits—why on earth would we turn to the market to solve a social problem--that is antithetical to its objective?

In sum, the world has changed, our solution for unemployment hasn't, and the result has been a disaster—i.e., as a result of the "Belief", above--nowhere in the OECD do we have ANY program SPECIFIC to ending unemployment!

Rather, our job creation is based on Republican "magical thinking"—i.e., we depend on jobs being created as a PRODUCT of something else happening—in this case, the success of the market—and, as noted, if the market fails, the jobless are out of luck!

And to illustrate just how far off base we are: We currently have a program--ostensibly to provide employment for seniors seeking some extra bucks to off-set the high cost of living—but rather than providing a job—the objective is to train seniors for a job in the Market—with training they don't need, and at 80, WHAT JOB? It is disingenuous for this program to hold out the offer of employment for seniors!

For perspective on the stubborn and sub-conscious nature of this "Belief" [3% is perceived as unsustainable, for example], ask: Why can we land on the Moon, but we can't fix unemployment? And why would we turn to anything as erratic as the market for a solution? And why do we ignore data which clearly tells us we are on the wrong path?

My solution is The Neighbor-To-Neighbor Job Creation Act [hereafter NTN]: A federally mandated, Social Insurance, owned by our employed, to provide a fund to hire/train our unemployed. For a modest 4% of salary policy cost we can create more "private-sector" jobs in 6 months, than our current path [HR 2847], in 6 years. Further, this has strong political support--86% of Americans believe that "anybody willing to work should be able to find a job...." [a quote from President Obama in "The Audacity of Hope"].

The market thrives when we have a robust, employed, consuming workforce--high unemployment/sluggish recovery is not a non sequitur. NTN is a "win-win" solution—The unemployed win, and the market wins.

Jim Green, Democrat candidate for Congress, 2000 www.Inclusivism.org jgreen5@satx.rr.com

(1) The Republican's job creation theory [asserted by Republicans as if it were fact] is cut taxes for the 1%, they will build factories with the windfall of cash—and we will all have a job in the corporation—it is BS—been there, did that—[Reaganomics] it has a 7 year shelf-life before the economy collapses [1987 & 2008], it drove us into a $10 trillion hole to dig out of, it cost the taxpayers $6 trillion more [and counting] to clean up their mess, and a 14.4 million job loss—In short, rather than being pro-market [which they boast] the Republican agenda is a MENACE to the market! And the "Belief", above, explains why Republicans spew out broad-brush, mean-spirited, irrational blather "The jobless are lazy", etc., etc.....

The lesson from Supply-Side is that we cannot siphon America's wealth away

from the consuming middle, without sending our economy into meltdown [and yet, it is the Republican *One and Only* program, to this day]! And, the Republican/Conservative propaganda that the government is an intrusive problem "and private enterprise a reliable solution" is both archaic and destructive in a 21st Century economy.

A BRIEF ADDENDUM: If one concludes that the market cannot provide everybody wanting a job, with a job—then they must look elsewhere to solve the problem of unemployment—and this, I believe, is the perceived conundrum faced by those charged with fixing our unemployment crisis—their *ONLY* choice is "public-sector" jobs, and many fear this will compete with "private-sector" jobs—but this is specious--for one, the employees are doing different things—and in the trade-off there is a far greater loss to the market by not employing an expanding and contracting public workforce [Buffer Stock Employment Model--Dr. William F. Mitchell, Australia]--that expands during downturns in the market and contracts as employees return to the private sector—[triggered at 3% under Humphrey-Hawkins].

And apparently least understood is that this is an **INDISPENSABLE,** *a sine quo non* component to the **EFFECTIVE** functioning of a modern market economy. Humphrey-Hawkins is Pro-Market—and they had it on the nose in limiting our unemployment to 3%.

And as just one illustration—were it not for the moneys from Social

Security Insurance [Social Insurance] in the U.S. percolating up through our economy during the 2008 meltdown, we would not be talking about having narrowly averted another Great Depression, we would be buried in one! A weapon, incidentally, available to President Obama, that was not available to FDR—and it also explains, in large part, why we have not had a Great Depression since.

And, perhaps it needs to be added that Social Insurance is democracy in its highest form. Cicero [106-43 BC] and reiterated by Christ "The people's good is the highest law"—and American citizens pooling their money for the common good—is DEMOCRACY, in fact--[some confused Republicans/Conservatives think the will of the American people is socialism, communism, or like blather, and evident by the current war against democracy by the Republicans in Congress—[i.e., the Republican's war against the will of the American people on gun control, as just one example]!

On a societal level, our choices are: Adapt and change in a world that is changing whether we like it or not—or create a Police State to hold anachronistic [unworkable] solutions in place....and in America, we have, sadly, opted for the latter....

Three vital components in creating a buffer stock of employees, include: 1] it would be based on the premise that we have far more work that needs to be done, than persons to fill these jobs ["make-work" jobs, is archaic thinking]. 2] It must have renewable funding [this is not a "jump-start" solution, as currently practiced], and 3] it will not add a dime to our deficit.

Finally, the notion that this would result in massive federal job creation is absurd, archaic—and HR 870 provides the correct model, with grants to local jurisdictions—and our local unemployment offices become employment offices.

To overcome this "Belief" we need to think differently, for instance, our mind-set should change from fix the market, and this will in turn fix unemployment—to fix unemployment, and this will fix the market. And our current anemic result in job creation is consummate proof of the fallacy that "market-only" solutions work [Ron Paul, et al]--it is a fallacy.

At present, American law still has one foot on the plantation--American "employees" are seen as "A Pool Of Slaves" [persons without rights—a slave by definition], to be used and discarded "at will"—

While conversely, the human need to be a productive member of society cannot be stressed strongly enough (2), and in time, in America, it will be looked upon as a Human Right—after all, our "economies" are only about one species—us—us human beings--it is one of the few things communism got right. If it isn't clear yet, I am a capitalist….I staunchly support: Make a better widget, sell it for a million bucks, and retire in South Florida— but the truth is, labels have become a menace and our political parties need to evolve into a single label, objective: "eclectic problem-solver"….[and a fitting label for President Obama—but undermined by our current political paralysis].

(2) Our current indifference to this human need is the reason for our epidemic of workplace violence, a pernicious incarceration rate, and our youth shooting each other at an alarming rate in every major city in America—and at the core of this indifference, and a plethora of other ills--is an anachronistic "BELIEF"….

Bio Info:
http://www.amazon.com/James-L.-Jim-Green/e/B001KHZIMM/ref=ntt_dp_e pwbk_0

See also: FULL EMPLOYMENT IS A PRO-MARKET CONCEPT, and ECONOMIC INCLUSIVISM: NEO-

CAPITALISM Inclusive Pro-Market Solutions For Our Social Problems, on Amazon/Kindle

PS: Apologize for the Caps [most software is not friendly with emphasis, where intended], and the length

CHAPTER THREE

President Obama/Council of Economic Advisers:

WHY WE CAN'T FIX UNEMPLOYMENT

Ignoring the "legal authorization" in 15 USC § 3101, is a lose-lose proposition—indeed, everyone loses—the Market, the unemployed, the politicians in Washington, the American people—

In brief, at no time should our unemployment in America exceed 3%--the above Public Law provides us with the legal authority to make it a fact—and the only thing standing in the way are myths, sacred cows, and a lack of imagination.

For the Council of Economic Advisers, indeed, all of our economic experts, today, to ignore this legal authority could be compared to when medicine sanctioned bleeding patients to cure illness—or when consensus had it that the world was flat....

World travel was out of the question when consensus had it that the world was flat....and our unemployment crisis faces the same dilemma, today, under our current mind-set.

And why we chose to continue failed Supply-Side job creation, is inexplicable! It is based on magical thinking, where the "promise of jobs" is falsely portrayed as the "certainty of jobs"—like a wish list to Santa Claus....[i.e., the "promise" is a lie perpetrated on the American people, and it is the Republican One and Only job creation solution, as I write—and which Democrats have obsequiously accepted]!

According to the CBO, on our current path it will be 2017 before we return to even an anemic 5.5%--with unemployment benefits already in jeopardy, and if the Market fails—the unemployed are out of luck!

Further, the market thrives when we have a robust, employed, consuming workforce—and, in large part, our manufacturing is disappearing because people do not buy the products manufactured for the Market—when they are unemployed....

And when 86% of Americans believe that "anybody willing to work should be able to find a job" there is solid political support for the "legal authorization" in 15 USC § 3101.

In sum, the world has changed, our job creation hasn't, and the result has been a disaster [the 2010 election which was retaliation for not fixing unemployment—and ushered in a House full of lunatics]....

See: FULL EMPLOYMENT IS A PRO-MARKET CONCEPT, on Amazon/Kindle

Jim Green, Democrat opponent to Lamar Smith, Congress, 2000

CHAPTER FOUR

THE HISTORY OF HOW WE GOT WHERE WE ARE:

In the mid-1970's, the colliding forces of automation, technology, globalization, etc., reached a critical mass—resulting in a Market no longer capable of producing the jobs necessary to its viability, and causing ubiquitous unemployment in all of the OECD countries--leaving their leaders conflicted, ever since, regarding the displaced employee. Eurozone unemployment is still in double digits, and Greece and Spain both in excess of 20%, plus. High unemployment was also a major factor in Arab Spring.

In the U.S., we took a pro-active role in addressing this economic shift—and in 1978 President Carter signed into law 15 USC § 3101--which "authorizes" the creation of a "reservoir of public employment" at any time our unemployment in America exceeds "3%".

In 1979, however, and in a panic over Humphrey-Hawkins—our ultra-conservative foundations, and desperate to promote the Supply-Side fraud, embraced a flawed paper by an obscure MIT student, David L. Birch "The Job Generation Process"; and [with lots of cash] gave his paper biblical importance, and every president since has cited his finding as gospel.

Birch's paper concluded that "small businesses" were the greatest generator of new jobs—problem is, for the purposes of policy-making—it is

BS. In a study at Harvard University in 2010, "The Myth of Small Business Job Creation" The research shows "no systematic relationship between firm size and growth." And that small businesses can actually detract from job growth.

In spite of this, however, Washington struggles, still, to make this antiquated notion, work--that it is only the market that can create jobs—and the result has been a disaster, politically as well as otherwise!

It would be impossible to still have 6.8% unemployment—if we were on the right path—and among other problems with this concept--if the market fails, the unemployed are out of luck.

Further, unemployment is a "social" problem we are seeking to address with a highly unstable, incompatible entity: The Market

What apparently isn't clear going forward is that an expanding and contracting public workforce is an *indispensable* component to the *effective* functioning of a modern market economy—

The market thrives when we have a robust, employed, consuming workforce—and overlooked is that HR 870, and the proposed "Neighbor-To-Neighbor Job Creation Act" www.Inclusivism.org [both authorized under Humphrey-Hawkins], are deficit-neutral--Pro-Market "win-win" solutions:

The American people win, and capitalism wins—

Jim Green, Democrat candidate for Congress, 2000

CHAPTER FIVE

COMMONS SENSE ECONOMICS

- **We cannot siphon America's wealth away from the consuming middle without causing economic collapse— [1987 & 2008—i.e., Supply-Side has a shelf-life of about 7 years before the economy goes into meltdown]--**
- **When every waking moment in capitalism is spent pondering ways to eliminate as many of us humans, as possible, from the workplace—to increase profits—why on earth would anyone in their right mind look to this model to solve an unemployment crisis?**
- **Unemployment is a "social" problem—and "our government" has an absolute responsibility to step forward with a viable solution.**

- We should never condemn the CEO who closes a plant when they are losing money—but we should be outraged by a government that is indifferent or incompetent in finding a viable solution to the resulting "social" problem.
- Capitalism thrives when we have a robust, employed, consuming public—
- "Public-sector" jobs is an accelerate to "private-sector" jobs—and will create more "private-sector" jobs in 6 months, than HR 2847 The HIRE Act, in 6 years, if ever—
- The belief that "public-sector" jobs can only be created by increasing the deficit, or equals a massive government program, such as WPA—is a belief that is suffering from a lack of imagination—
- The Humphrey-Hawkins Full Employment Act which authorizes

the creation of a "reservoir of public employment" anytime our unemployment in America rises above "3%" is a Pro-Market solution—and an INDISPENSABLE tool for economic survival in a modern market economy—See also HR 870 [currently in Committee]--

- In the mid-1970's—the colliding forces of automation, globalization, innovation, etc., reached a critical mass, resulting in ubiquitous unemployment—and has left our leaders befuddled with what to do with the displaced employee?
- Our response in America was H-H, above, in 1978—but inexplicably never implemented—and the resulting high unemployment cost Carter the election in 1980--
- "Most [Americans think] that anybody willing to work should be able to find a job." President

Obama, "The Audacity of Hope" – it is not the American people standing the in the way our implementing H-H—it is bad advice—

- The correlation between high unemployment and our lethargic economy is absolute—

- A comprehensive public employment program, in compliance with H-H, such a HR 870, or a federally mandated, mutual insurance, owned by America's employed--to hire/train our unemployed [www.Inclusivism.org]: Is Pro-Market, and pro-the American people--

Jim Green, Democrat candidate for Congress, 2000

PS For clarity, I am a capitalist—I strongly advocate for: build a better widget, sell it for a million bucks, and

retire in South Florida—and the path we are on now is _Anti-Market!_

CHAPTER SIX

A FEW WORDS ABOUT AN ERRONEOUS "BELIEF":

This book is how "belief systems" have prevented us from solving our unemployment crisis—has undermined our market economy, and has left us with 25 million unemployed/underemployed Americans—but the belief where we went off the rails—for instance, caused one zany Republican congressman to claim that males masturbate in the womb--is the "belief" that "sex is a sin"—and we took a very "natural and healthy" part of our life, and made it "dirty and nasty"—the following sums up this dilemma.....

[I couldn't resist including this...and yes I am the author.....]

A MESSAGE FROM GOD

MANY CENTURIES AGO, a man of the cloth, we don't know his name, and in a flash of insight (perhaps induced by peyote) told his flock that "sex is a sin". And lo and behold he learned that by taking a very natural and healthy part of our life and turning it into something that was "dirty and nasty", that he could imprison his flock, and fill his coffers, and hallelujah it was a great day for the Lord!

Quickly, his miracle spread to other churches in his village, and then to the next village, and then the next county, and then state, and soon it spread to all the churches in the ancient world, and all of their flocks cowed in fear and shame and became imprisoned, and their coffers over-floweth. Hallelujah, it was a great day for the Lord!

And to keep the myth alive they started inventing stories, half-baked stories, that made no sense to anyone who is rational, such as "Mary was a virgin"—well, she just had to be a virgin because she would never partake in anything that was dirty and nasty, like sex (if you're doing it right), and this was necessary to make "sex is a sin" make sense...so they invented a Mary that was "sinless"--you get the picture. And their coffers over-floweth. Hallelujah, it was a great day for the Lord!

No one seemed to be bothered that when we play tricks on the human mind by taking something that is very natural and healthy, such as sex, and make it dirty and nasty that all kinds of bad things happen to the human mind:

Such as most pedophiles, and most serial killers, and voting Republican, and unwarranted suicides, and most mental illness, and unwanted pregnancies. (Teens not wanting to have sex is the perversion, not the other way around, and by replacing sex education and condoms, with unrealistic "abstinence", and by using blather about "low self-esteem" to shame them into not "sinning"—We have a teen pregnancy in the U.S. twice that of England and Canada!).

But none of this mattered, because their coffers over-floweth, and

Hallelujah, it is a great day for the Lord!

There is a cure--------Tell these right-wing loonies to shove it....

GOD

CHAPTER SEVEN

86% OF AMERICANS AGREE WITH HUMPHREY-HAWKINS TO END OUR UNEMPLOYMENT CRISIS

For the past 65 years we have had two parallel paths to address unemployment in America—

To assure employment for our troops returning from WW II, President Truman signed into law "The Full Employment Act of 1946"—

This was expanded upon in 1978 with the "Humphrey-Hawkins Full Employment Act", signed into law by President Carter—

And HR 870 is a 21st Century version of this path to full employment in America.

Humphrey-Hawkins best defines this path to addressing unemployment in America--and it authorizes our government to create a "reservoir of public employment" anytime our unemployment rises above "3%" [and we are still over twice the percent necessary to trigger this Public Law, five years into our recovery].

And in spite of the fact that this path to employment has been the law of the land since 1946—and is a Pro-Market solution---Washington has lacked the wherewithal to implement this path to employment on behalf of the American people—[a point not lost on the "occupy" movement].

Rather, Washington has taken the alternate parallel path—by insisting that human labor is a "component" in the free enterprise system—[barely distinguishable from the machine the human operates] to be used and discarded "at will"—and that it is an attack upon "freedom" to challenge this concept, but whose "freedom"?

As a result, however, "conventional wisdom" has insisted that it is the market, alone, that can fix our unemployment crisis—the result has been a disaster—

The market thrives when we have a robust, employed, consuming public— and by taking this parallel path—we not only have a staggering 7.4% unemployment rate, but a struggling recovery as well.

Ironically, following WW II, Australia passed a law very similar to our Full Employment Act of 1946—

Difference is—they actually put it into effect—and over the next 30 years— [until the cold winds of conservatism swept in Reagan and Thatcher, etc.] – the government in Australia saw as a solemn responsibility that "anybody willing to work should be provided with a job." [a quote from the "Audacity of Hope"—regarding a belief held by most Americans].

The citizens of Australia still refer to this 30 years as their "Golden Age".

The puzzlement for America: When the vast majority of Americans [86% by one poll] agree with this alternate path to full employment—why does Washington refuse to enforce a Public

Law we have on the books for the benefit of the America people?

We are a democracy, aren't we?

Jim Green, Democrat candidate for Congress, 2000 www.Inclusivism.org

CHAPTER EIGHT

I didn't write the following. It is a cut and paste from FACEBOOK, or some blog [would like to give credit if knew the author]--but it is so on target regarding how "fear" is driving Conservative policy in America today—i.e., is undermining America and our progress—and relegating America to a Third World country status, rather than a world leader— FDR had it on the nose in "All we have to fear, is fear itself"…at his inaugural in 1933….

"Conservatives are such cowards: they are afraid of gay people getting married or serving in the military; they are afraid of bringing terrorists to super max prisons in the US from which no one has ever escaped; they are afraid of the boy scouts letting gay kids in; they are afraid of everyone voting and are constantly suppressing the vote under some bogus voter fraud theory; they are afraid of letting students vote at their universities; they are afraid of women having the right to choose; they even are afraid of women getting contraception [the real issue actually is a women's agency and control over their bodies]; they are afraid of immigration reform leading to citizenship because they are afraid of-- name whatever reason; they are afraid of mandating gun purchasers to undergo background checks for crazy people and terrorists; they are afraid of people smoking pot; they are afraid of climate change being real and contradicting their beloved Bible; they are afraid of legitimate campaign reform; they are afraid of Muslims; they are afraid of blacks; they are afraid of atheists; they are afraid of hippies; they are afraid of socialists; they are probably still afraid of monsters under their beds; they are just rank cowards and keep making things up to be afraid of."

CHAPTER NINE

The following may appear to be out of place, or irrelevant to the title—but it is, in fact, highly relevant—if government officials were criminally negligent in the death of a news paper editor's son, as retaliation for an editorial he had written—and the violation of his First Amendment rights would fly off these pages—but superimpose those exact facts over our rights as an "employee" in America— and our rights become invisible— Indeed, even disregarding the almost unbelievable circumstance, here, when I was fraudulently stripped of my constitutional rights in America, by a former Hitler Youth [and unfortunately, all true]. The larger point being: We will never be able to end unemployment in America so long as we cease to be American citizens, when we go to work....

Please Forward to AG Holder:

AFFIDAVIT

In 1935, Hitler made it legal to deny rights of citizenship to all persons who were Jewish...in short, Hitler dehumanized the Jews in Germany....laying the groundwork for all kinds of atrocities to be perpetrated on persons of the Jewish faith.

A year later William W Schwarzer became a Hitler Youth, and as a condition, pledged his allegiance to Hitler.

I am a U.S. citizen. As a result, I am guaranteed as a matter of that citizenship certain protected rights under the U.S. Constitution.

As documented in **THE HARVARD BOYS CLUB [B&N]**, Federal Judge Schwarzer stripped me of my U.S. citizenship, by lying in federal court record C77-0307-WWS--with the **SPECIFIC INTENT** to deny a Legal Remedy when my protected legal rights under the U.S. Constitution, were violated….

AND, with his full knowledge that our six year old son, who is now dead, might still be alive if my constitutional rights had not been violated!

In short, Schwarzer was also covering up **CRIMINAL NEGLIGENCE** on the part of the government Defendants in this action.

I filed a COMPLAINT FOR FRAUD against Federal Judge Schwarzer [unique in American jurisprudence], which to this day, the federal judiciary has yet to find without merit. [If my Complaint was without merit–the federal judiciary would have declared it to be frivolous in a New York second—and that has never happened]….

Also, in the court record you will find—to the shock of a packed court room, and myself--I shouted at Schwarzer, on the Bench "I am a U.S. citizen, I have rights under the U.S. Constitution"----and all the more remarkable because at the time I had yet to learn that Schwarzer was born in Berlin, Germany on 4-30-25, had spent his formative years under the adverse influence of the Third Reich, and was a Hitler Youth.

When a U.S. citizen is denied a Legal Remedy when their rights under the U.S. Constitution are violated [particularly as a product of Fraud]— they cease to be an American citizen…the certainty of a Legal Remedy when our rights are violated is the glue that makes us a free people.

Without a Legal Remedy—the Bill of Rights becomes a toothless tiger….worthless [and Schwarzer's Fraud applies to EVERY citizen in America under the Equal Protection clause]—and that is the Legal Imperative raised, here-- Schwarzer's Fraud is not acceptable in America, not once—NOT EVER!

I certify the above to be true and correct under penalty of perjury.

/S/Jim Green, Democrat candidate for Congress, 2000

CHAPTER TEN

IF WORK, THE RIGHT TO BE A PRODUCTIVE HUMAN, BECAME THE "LEGAL RIGHT" OF EACH CITIZEN OF LEGAL AGE—WHAT WOULD HAPPEN-- [A FUTURISTIC FABLE, OR FUTURE FACT]?

First, an "employment insurance" [Social Insurance] would be established to provide a fund to hire/train our unemployed. Our unemployment offices would become employment offices, and work could not be denied to any citizen who applies.

At present there is a superficial interest on the part of our unemployment offices in finding work for the unemployed—but by and large they are another of our antiquated Police State solutions, and they see their real role as acting as a police agency in denying claims to save money for "employers", corporate and public, and to be vigilant in checking up to see that unemployment recipients are not cheating. Most believe that the recipients are lazy and don't want to work.

All of this, including the erroneous assumptions about humans, would disappear—because the need for unemployment payments, as well as most of our current welfare system, and Food Stamps would be greatly reduced, or disappear-- and the saved taxes would be returned to the "employment insurance" pool set up to provide employment for the unemployed.

Also, funding would come from the proposed deficit-neutral Neighbor-To-Neighbor Job Creation Act [or like program], and we could reduce our unemployment to 3% [be in compliance with 15 USC § 3101], within a year of becoming law.

This insurance would be federally mandated, much the same as Social Security Insurance, and auto insurance, if one works in America, enrollment would be mandatory [the same as auto insurance]—even for the president---

In short, every person who works would pay into the insurance in the interest of providing employment to those who are unemployed—and while there may a disgruntled soul here and there (who do not want their money used to employ someone who is black, or brown, or old—there always is) it is speculated that their numbers are miniscule, and this would be wildly applauded by the vast majority in the interest of the larger society—and in their own self-interest, should fate tap them on the shoulder. 86% of Americans believe that "anybody willing to work should be able to find a job".

The lesson from Social Security Insurance is that we have not had another Great Depression since it was implemented in 1940, and that Social Security and Military Retirement moneys, etc., trickling up through our economy is most likely the reason we are not in one now. In short, finding work to be a "legal right" is a "win-win" proposition, and it cannot be ignored that Bill Gates became the richest man in the world, in large part, as a result of Social Security funds percolating up through our economy.

There are currently 8,800 pending state infrastructure programs seeking funding in the respective states, so there is hardly a shortage of employment opportunities. Our emphasis, of course, should be on those projects which will make America energy independent and on protecting the environment.

And we should not rule out allowing the owners of the, above, "employment insurance" to vote on national projects—such as a high speed rail system, etc., ---and dividends would be paid to the owners of the employment insurance from unused funds. This is, after all, not a tax----it is an insurance plan.

Finally, it cannot be stressed strongly enough that The right to work and be a productive citizen was a given in primitive societies, but lost in the age of industrialization and advent of the corporation,—and in the end it may have more of a psychological, than economic impact—because over time it will change the way we look at each other.

Jim Green, Democrat candidate for Congress, Dist 21, TX, 2000
www.Inclusivism.org

CHAPTER ELEVEN

TO THE READER: Given you have gotten this far, and agree with the proposed changes—and particularly given the pernicious Citizens United—our democracy, and the above, or any, progress, will be in peril absent a "fail-safe" electronic voting system. The following is my proposed solution, and like every solution proposed, here, feed-back--your proposed improvement, etc. is welcomed:

THE FAIL-SAFE ELECTRONIC VOTING ACT

So long as the potential for manipulation of electronic voting continues to exist—our elections in America will be in peril! In spite of all the polls showing a strong Obama

victory--it was not until 10 PM Central on 11-4-08.....that we could breath a sigh of relief....we had been cheated out of the past two elections....with many believing that Bush was never legally elected president of the United States....and we were braced for the worst.......this can, and MUST be fixed before 2016, so that this never happens again, and in the interest of all who support fair and open elections--regardless of party. Accordingly, it is urged that we adopt the following:

1) EVERY electronic voting machine (hereafter EVM), must be inexpensive, identical throughout the U.S. in a 1/150 ratio, and *must count and produce a hard-copy of the recorded votes*. In addition, an extra copy of their recorded votes would be produced (not necessarily a hard-copy), marked "Voter's Copy", and

containing "NOTICE: Do Not Destroy Until Every Election On Your Ballot Is Certified". [If Wal-Mart handed us a piece of paper with the words "trust us" as a receipt for our purchases—we would be outraged—and this is our current electronic voting nightmare—but in this case it is our democracy at risk]!

2) *After confirming that their votes are recorded correctly*, the voter would then insert the hard-copy ballot into a software-free (count only) optical scanner (hereafter OS), for a second count. The hard-copy ballot would be retained by election officials in the event a candidate asks for a recount (*not possible under the current system, and which undermines the legality of each such election*). The EVM and the OS must be manufactured by different companies (which is universally true

today).

3) Election officials assigned to oversee the EVM, would be prevented by law from overseeing the OS, and vice-versa, and stiff criminal penalties would be imposed for violations.

4) Further, every EVM would be programmed with raw data re the total registration rolls, by party, and norms for their voting history, etc.,---- as an "alert" to a possible irregularity, such as an "under-vote"—or "vote-flipping" etc., and *standards* established to suspend certification where there is an "improbable result", at least temporarily, of a particular election until the discrepancy is cleared up. (This is what computers do best, and it would be very easy to create such a program).

5) At the end of the election day, tallies would be taken from the EVM and the OS, for each candidate. _If the tallies didn't balance for any given election, or if there is an "alert", that election cannot be certified until the "error" is corrected._ **If the candidates agree (the victory is certain), minor discrepancies in the count could be disregarded. While probably rare, the Voter, or a random sample of Voters, would be required by law to return their Copy of the recorded votes to the election office to clear up any "error", or where an "alert" signals the need for same.**

6) Further, every state provides for a recount when the total vote falls below a certain percent of difference between the candidates, impossible to conduct with the current EVM. And thus Congress must mandate the following

regarding presidential candidates: A RUN-OFF election is mandated and triggered in those states where the percent of total vote is less than .5% of difference between the two candidates; said election to be held on the second Saturday following the election, on PAPER BALLOTS ONLY, and contain ONLY the names of the relevant candidates, for instance: "Barack Obama, Democrat" and "John McCain, Republican"—with oversight in counting by a representative(s) of each party—said procedure providing more than adequate time to meet the Electoral College mandate [Ideally, all of this could be eliminated if we did away with the Electoral College, but until then….]. NOTE: Had this been the law in 2000, Al Gore would be our president, and America would have been spared the economic, etc.,

disaster that followed!

7) Finally, absent the above safeguards, and until these safeguards are in place--Congress must mandate that PAPER BALLOTS, ONLY, can be used in our presidential elections. This is not a "partisan" issue, it is a "pro-democracy" issue. Most importantly, this will return the responsibility for our elections, and our vote counting, back into the hands of the individual voter, where it belongs, and out of the hands of "corporate control"---_it is_ _after all "our democracy", itself, that is at risk if we don't take these steps---and in that regard, is there any time or cost differential that is too great?_

Jim Green

ABOUT THE AUTHOR: I was employed in our Criminal Justice System for a cumulative 20 years as a probation officer, with 5 of those years as a chief probation officer. I authored the concept of "Shock Incarceration" which became law in Kansas in 1970, and then was adopted in numerous jurisdictions in the U.S. and also spread to Europe—it is currently identified in the U.S. as "Boot Camp" [as the means to "shock" the young offender—and a total distortion of my original intent—like many ideas, once released, they take on a life of their own]. I also instigated establishment of the first Court Psychiatric Clinic in the U.S., in conjunction with psychiatrists from the Menninger Foundation, as a chief probation officer. Finally, I was the Democrat candidate for Congress, District 21,

TX, 2000. I would most define myself as a Social Ecologist-- [albeit my degree is in Psychology]. My web page is www.Inclusivism.org –which has been on the internet since 1996.

A BRIEF ADDENDUM: When the U.S. Supreme Court denied certiorari—where the violation of my constitutional rights were obvious, and criminal negligence on the part of the government defendants in the death of our son, equally obvious—I filed a Petition for Rehearing [which is automatic]—and included the following. The Clerk of the U.S.

Supreme Court called me at my work in California, and asked that I withdraw the "cartoon" [a reprint from The NEW YORKER] from my Petition. I refused on the basis of the First Amendment, and it remains in the archives at the U.S. Supreme Court [Docket #: 79-1627], to this day. The wording [not that clear] is: "Excellent, excellent. A fine blend of truths, half-truths, and blatant falsehoods".

IN THE

Supreme Court of the United States

October Term, 1979

No. 79-1627

JAMES L. GREEN,

Petitioner,

VS.

OTHER BOOKS BY THIS AUTHOR ON AMAZON/KINDLE/BN:

- THE HARVARD BOYS CLUB: Hitler's Assault On Our Freedoms From His Grave
- MY LETTERS TO PRESIDENT OBAMA: Confessions Of A Compulsive Letter Writer
- OUR GREED AND IGNORANCE: Poses A Far Greater Threat To America, Than Terrorism
- LETTERS ON STEROIDS: Confessions Of A Compulsive Letter-To-The-Editor Writer
- THE FIRST TIME I HAD SEX: And, The Religious Intolerance Attack On America
- WHY PRESIDENT OBAMA LOST THE 2012 ELECTION: A Wake-Up Call

- ECONOMIC INCLUSIVISM: Neo-Capitalism/An Anthology: Inclusive pro-market solutions to our social problems
- AMERICA IS ONE SICK MF: Why Greed-Driven America Went Off The Rails....
- EVERY GIVEN SUNDAY: A Scientific Formula To Predict NFL Games